DIVORCED, NOT DEFEATED

DIVORCED, NOT DEFEATED

RUBY CROTTY

J3 Publishers, LLC

Divorced, Not Defeated

Published by J3 Publishers, LLC in Jacksonville, FL

Cover art and graphics by: Ruby Crotty and Designs by Jobi-www.designsbyjobi.com

Concept by Ruby Crotty

Author photo by Lyndsay Almeida-www.lyndsayalmeida.com

ISBNs: 978-0-9787374-6-7 (paperback) 978-0-9787374-7-4 (eBook)

Printed in the United States of America

space for readers not just to consume information, but to genuinely sit with the Lord in their healing process. Ruby writes with honesty, humility, clarity, and compassion. Her words feel like they were written by someone who has truly walked through fire and discovered that God remains faithful in the middle of it. I am genuinely celebrating this resource because I believe it will help many people feel seen while also lovingly leading them back toward truth, healing, and intimacy with Jesus. If you are navigating divorce, separation, grief, regret, confusion, or the long road of rebuilding, this book will remind you that while divorce may be part of your story, it does not get to define your identity. Most importantly, this book reminds readers of a truth many desperately need to hear: God does not pull away from brokenness. He draws near to it."

April Lynn Terrell – Care Minister, The Church of Eleven22

"As a publisher and editor, we see many good manuscripts, but it's a rarity to see one that, as you read and correct, you stop, grab a tissue, pray, and even implement the truths you're reading. Ruby's book is sure to not only speak truth to men and women who have gone through divorce but also be used as a tool in God's hand to heal their broken hearts and revive their souls. This book will encourage all readers to keep moving forward, because anyone who has suffered a divorce can walk in the reality that yes, they're divorced, but NOT defeated."

Jobi Jones – Co-Founder of J3 Publishers, LLC

"Information alone doesn't change our lives; application does. And this book is exactly that. *Divorced, Not Defeated* is a powerful reminder that God meets us exactly where we are, but He loves us too much to leave us there. Through biblical truth, wisdom, and heartfelt transparency, Ruby walks alongside the reader through some of life's darkest valleys and seasons with both grace and strength. This study doesn't just offer encouragement; it offers perspective, healing, and hope. It reminds us that our pain is not our identity, our circumstances are not our future, and divorce does not get the final say. God does."

Carrie Fuentes – Founder of Kingdom Misfits

Praise for Divorced, Not Defeated

“Hearing what God spoke to Ruby at one of our Gatherings is the heartbeat of why Rivers of Eden Ministries exists. Watching her walk out, her “GO” has been the overflow. Ruby’s heart is devoted to Jesus and his people. This book is founded on biblical truth, and I know it will transform and heal lives for the glory of God. It is an honor to call Ruby a friend and a partner on the mission field.”

Lindsey Sima – Founder of Rivers of Eden Ministries

"I had the honor of reading an early sample of Divorced, Not Defeated by Ruby Crotty, and I can honestly say this is one of the most biblically grounded, pastorally tender, and emotionally honest resources I have read on divorce and healing. As someone who is also divorced, I especially appreciate the way Ruby approaches this topic with both truth and compassion. She does not minimize the pain, grief, confusion, regret, or devastation that divorce can bring, but she also refuses to leave people buried under shame. That balance matters deeply. What stood out to me immediately is that this book does not abandon biblical truth in an attempt to comfort hurting people. Ruby somehow holds both wisdom and grace. She honors the holiness of the covenant while also reminding wounded people that God’s mercy, compassion, and nearness have not left them. This is not a book filled with clichés, shallow encouragement, or self-help language wrapped in Christian terminology. It consistently points people back to the character of God, the truth of Scripture, and the healing found only in Jesus Christ. As someone who has spent years walking with people through grief, trauma, heartbreak, and restoration in ministry, I deeply appreciate the pastoral tone woven throughout these pages. The reflective questions, prayers, and Scripture invitations create

"One of the most powerful things about this book is that it doesn't avoid the hard truths; it doesn't stay in shallow water, but courageously steps into deeper places with biblical wisdom, honesty, compassion, and hope. Ruby reminds readers that God is not intimidated by brokenness and that healing begins when we stop hiding, face what's real, and allow His truth to reshape our hearts and lives. This book is a beautiful invitation to let God meet you in the waves and lead you toward deeper healing, freedom, and restoration through Christ."

Kadi Baker – Founder, Faithfully Brewed

"As a divorced mom of three, this book hit me deeply. The truth is not watered down, nor is it weaponized. This book creates space for people to acknowledge the pain and reality of divorce while still reminding them they are fully loved, seen, and redeemable by God. So many people either speak about divorce with shame and condemnation or with complete dismissal of the covenant itself. This book manages to hold both truth and grace in the same hand, and that is rare. Ruby's words are honest, grounded, biblically sound, and deeply compassionate. I think this book is going to help a lot of hurting people stop seeing themselves as "disqualified" and start seeing themselves as still chosen, still loved, and still capable of healing and purpose. There were multiple moments I had to stop reading simply because I felt so understood. Thank you for being willing to write about something so painful with so much courage, wisdom, and tenderness."

Jenni Boyer – Divorced Mom of Three, Entrepreneur

"...Ruby's poignant way of navigating how the Lord hates divorce, but not the divorced, while still pointing the reader towards marriage as a good gift from above, is incredible. Her words towards the audience are convicting in the best way. As it says in 1 Corinthians, "Be watchful, stand firm in the faith, act like men, be strong," and in 1 Peter, "Be sober-minded, be watchful". This book will help you to be more watchful in how you approach a Godly marriage, how to be purposeful in being single, and how to give yourself grace because JESUS DOES!

Daniel L. Middlebrooks II – Youth Leader and Friend

"Ruby does a beautiful job balancing truth and love in *Divorced, Not Defeated*. She does not shy away from sharing God's truth about how He hates divorce, not the person, while also pointing readers to His incredible grace, mercy, and redemption. In my ministry, helping women who have experienced trafficking, trauma, and exploitation, I often meet women who feel too far gone for God. I can see how that same heartbreak and feeling of defeat can happen through divorce as well. But God. There is always hope, healing, and restoration in Him. Nothing is impossible for God. If you have found yourself feeling defeated because of divorce, no matter the circumstances, then allow these pages to remind you that your story is not over. God still brings beauty from ashes, and new hope and new life are waiting for you in Him."

Tiffany Brearton – Author of "From Stilettos To Grace" and "From A Mess To His Message," Co-Founder of She Was Made For More Ministries

For the ones who thought the ending was the end, it wasn't.

Contents

Introduction

The marriage is over! And, for some, it feels like drowning. For others, it feels like finally coming up for air.

Regardless of where you stand today, gasping for breath or breathing freely, we are here, together. Not alone. Divorced, yes. Defeated, no.

The truth is, whether we are struggling to keep our heads above water or learning to walk in freedom, the road ahead is long and winding. No one stands at the altar thinking about the day it will all come crashing down. No one rocks a newborn to sleep and dreams about dismantling the life they built. But it happens.

Sometimes it's sudden. Sometimes it's a slow unraveling. Sometimes it's a choice we never thought we'd have to make. And sometimes it's a choice that was made for us.

But here's what I know: what happened may shape you, but it does not get to define you. This is not the end of your story.

If you know me, you know I don't shy away from the truth. I'm open, honest, and I lead with it, even when it's hard to hear. Not because I want to offend you, but because I love you enough to care more about your healing, your freedom, and your identity in Christ than your comfort. And if you get a little mad at me along the way, don't worry, it usually doesn't last long.

If you don't know me, hi, I'm Ruby.

I'm a daughter of God before anything else. I'm also divorced, just like you.

I've been given the gift of motherhood to a daughter and a son who keep me grounded while reminding me to keep dreaming. I love God, I love His Word, and I love walking with people as they step into the wholeness only Jesus can give.

After 18 years in dentistry, God called me into a completely different direction. I stepped into the mental health space for a season, and then pivoted again into Christian leadership. If there's one thing I've learned, it's this: obedience doesn't always look linear, and that's okay. God is not intimidated by your transitions; He leads through them.

I'm a strategist at heart, a worshipper in spirit, and a firm believer in kitchen karaoke. I've walked through enough valleys to know the view is worth it at the top. I've laughed when I should've cried, and cried when I thought I had nothing left. I believe in grace without compromise, hope without apology, and truth without sugarcoating. And because of that, we're going to start this journey with something I call HARD TRUTHS.

These aren't meant to shame you, condemn you, or keep you stuck. They are meant to shine light into the places we would rather avoid, because truth is the only thing strong enough to break chains. Before we can rebuild, we must face what's real.

Each section of this book is designed to walk you through that process. You won't just read, you'll engage, and after every section, you'll find: A short prayer to help you surrender what you're processing to God, scriptures to anchor you in truth, not emotion. And reflection questions to help you sit with what God is revealing, so that you can apply it to your life.

This is where the work happens, not in rushing through pages, but in allowing God to meet you right where you are. So, take a deep breath, and let's get started.

I'm going to love you through this, but I'm also going to tell you the truth.

In His Love,

Ruby

HARD TRUTH #1
YES, GOD HATES DIVORCE. NO, HE DOESN'T HATE YOU.

Let's rip the band-aid off. God's Word is clear, He hates divorce (Malachi 2:16), but He doesn't hate you. That's a big distinction we must get straight before we can move forward in healing. Divorce breaks God's heart because of what it does to His children, in that it causes pain, broken trust, and families being torn apart. But His love for you? That hasn't changed one bit. In this section, we're going to unpack this truth, confront the lies that creep in, and learn how to stand in the freedom of His grace.

Chapter 1

God's Heart About Divorce

Malachi 2:16

Please understand that God hates the pain, betrayal, and brokenness, not the person.

The Bible says it plainly: "For I hate divorce!" says the Lord, the God of Israel (Malachi 2:16 NLT).

You can't water that down, reframe it, or dress it up in a bow. God hates divorce. And I'll be honest. The first time I read that, my heart sank. It's not an easy verse to swallow when you've lived through it. For many of us, it stirs up questions, doubts, and even guilt. Maybe you felt relief instead of shame. Maybe you knew it was the right decision, but still wrestled with whether you had disappointed God.

Here's the thing. Divorce is never God's best for us. Marriage was designed as a covenant, a living picture of His faithful love for His people (Ephesians 5:31–32). But we live in a fallen world, and sin fractures what God intended to be whole. Because of that, divorce happens. Sometimes through betrayal. Sometimes through abandonment. Sometimes it's because we didn't have faith, the right tools, or an understanding at the time to protect the covenant. And sometimes, divorce happens because we entered a marriage God never asked us to enter.

For some of us, the warning signs were there long before the wedding day. Wise counsel spoke up. Premarital counselors raised concerns. Family and friends said, "Something's not right." And for a variety of reasons, such as fear of being alone, pressure, infatuation, trauma, or simply not knowing God well enough yet, we ignored or silenced those voices.

Not every marriage is put together by God. God honors covenant, but He also gives us free will. And when we choose outside of His wisdom, the consequences can be devastating. A marriage built in disobedience or blindness often becomes a place of confusion, dysfunction, and deep pain. Many of those marriages eventually end in divorce. Yes, God can redeem some of those marriages. He absolutely can. But if you are holding this book, chances are you already know the outcome of yours. This is not hypothetical for you. This was your story.

Acknowledging that truth is not about shame. It is about clarity. And clarity is the beginning of healing. Acknowledging that divorce happens is not the same as saying it is okay or that it does not matter. It matters deeply to God. So much so that He tells us plainly how much He hates it. But His hatred of divorce comes from love for His children and grief over the pain it causes, not from anger toward the people who have walked through it.

There's a reason God addresses divorce so directly in Scripture, and it is not to shame us. God does not name things in His Word to condemn His children. He names them to protect them. Every boundary He gives is an act of love. Every warning is meant to spare us from harm, not push us into hiding.

When God speaks about divorce, He is not standing over you in judgment. He is standing in front of you, saying, "I see where this leads, and I do not want this pain for you." His heart has always been to provide protection, not punishment. He hates what divorce does to His children. He hates the way it shatters trust. He hates the tears cried behind closed doors. He hates the way it rips families in half, strains finances, and bruises souls. He hates the bitterness, shame, and loneliness that creep in when a covenant is broken. If you have been left, betrayed, or abandoned, His heart breaks with yours (Psalm 34:18).

If you were the one who left because of abuse, adultery, or a covenant already shattered beyond repair, His heart still breaks with yours, even if you left for reasons that do not look "big enough" to others. Maybe your spouse did not want to work on the marriage. Maybe you did not know God at the time and did not understand what a covenant meant. Maybe you ignored wise counsel back then, and you are only now seeing it clearly in hindsight.

Here is the truth. Sin and brokenness show up in a thousand different ways, and God's grace covers all of them (Romans 5:20). Your divorce does not get graded on a scale where some are forgivable and others are not. It is not a pass-or-fail test where you only "count" if you have the right reason. Divorce is always the result of living in a fallen world, and Jesus came for all of it: the sin, the brokenness, and the lost. (Luke 19:10).

God is not looking down at you with crossed arms and a scowl. He is not tallying up your failures to hold against you. He is the Father who runs to meet you on the road back home (Luke 15:20). The same God who hates divorce is the God who promises, "There is no condemnation for those who belong to Christ Jesus" (Romans 8:1).

This is the starting point of healing. Accept the truth. God hates divorce. Accept the bigger truth. He loves you enough to redeem the wreckage. You are not defined by the end of your marriage. You are defined by the One who conquered the grave to call you His own (1 Peter 2:9).

Let's Pray Together

Father,

You see every part of my story, the pain, the questions, and the places I still carry shame. Thank You that You are not disappointed in me, but near to me. Help me to receive the truth that there is no condemnation for me in Christ. Where I have believed lies about who I am or how You see me, replace them with Your truth. Give me clarity, give me peace, and begin healing the places that still hurt. Teach me to see You as You truly are, a good Father who loves me.

In Jesus' name,

Amen.

Sit With These Scriptures

"There is therefore now no condemnation for those who are in Christ Jesus." Romans 8:1

"The Lord is close to the brokenhearted and saves those who are crushed in spirit." Psalm 34:18

SIT IN THAT TRUTH
GOD'S HEART ABOUT DIVORCE

Take a few moments to ask God to remove any distractions and to silence your own voice and the enemy's voice, so that you can hear God clearly and focus on Him. Invite the Holy Spirit to help you as you work through these questions.

1. When you read that God hates divorce, what did it stir in you: guilt, relief, confusion, or something else? Be honest about why.

2. Have you been seeing God as disappointed in you, or as a Father who still delights in you? What shaped that view?

3. Looking back on your story, where can you now begin to see clarity, whether in your choices, in your circumstances, or in what you didn't understand at the time?

4. Have you been carrying shame about your divorce in a way that is shaping how you see yourself or how you approach God?

5. Do you truly believe that your story falls under "no condemnation" (Romans 8:1), or do you feel like your situation is different? Why?

Chapter 2

Loved Beyond Measure

Romans 8:38-39

Nothing can separate you from His love. Hey friend, if you only hear one thing today, let it be this: God's love for you on your worst day is the same as it is on your best day. Divorce doesn't make Him love you less. Your mistakes don't make Him flinch. Your tears don't make Him pull away. You are still fully known and fully loved.

The Bible says, "Nothing can ever separate us from God's love. Neither death nor life, neither angels nor demons, neither our fears for today nor our worries about tomorrow—not even the powers of hell can separate us from God's love" (Romans 8:38 NLT). Notice it doesn't say "nothing except divorce." There is no fine print that disqualifies you.

The enemy would love for you to believe God has pulled back because of what's happened, that He's standing at a distance, arms crossed, waiting for you to "fix yourself" before He comes close again. But that's not the God of the Bible.

Psalm 103:8 says, "The Lord is compassionate and merciful, slow to get angry and filled with unfailing love." His love is not performance-based; it's covenant-based. And unlike human covenants that can be broken, His covenant love toward you cannot be undone.

Think about it, the disciples abandoned Jesus in His darkest hour, yet He still came back to them after the resurrection with words of peace, not punishment (John 20:1920). That's the kind of love He has for you. He's not avoiding you; He's running toward you.

But hear me, His grace does not excuse poor behavior. His love is not permission to stay stuck in the same patterns that led to destruction. When we truly grasp His relentless love for us, it should stir something deep within us, a desire to heal, to grow, to forgive, and to become more like Christ (2 Corinthians 5:17, Romans 12:2). Grace is a gift, but it's also an invitation. An invitation to step out of the ashes and into transformation.

So, when the guilt creeps in and when the enemy whispers, "You messed up too badly for God to love you like before," then call it what it is, a lie. Stand on the truth that God's love is steady, sure, and unchanging. Let that truth push you toward wholeness in Him.

Let's Pray Together

Father,

Thank You that Your love for me is not based on my performance, my past, or my mistakes. Thank You that nothing, absolutely nothing, can separate me from Your love. When I feel distant, remind me that You have not moved. When lies try to take root, help me recognize them and replace them with Your truth. Teach me to receive Your love fully and to live from that place of love. Stir in me a desire to grow, to heal, and to become more like You.

In Jesus' name,

Amen.

Sit With These Scriptures

"For I am convinced that neither death nor life, neither angels nor demons, neither the present nor the future, nor any powers... will be able to separate us from the love of God that is in Christ Jesus our Lord." Romans 8:38–39

"The Lord is compassionate and merciful, slow to get angry and filled with unfailing love." Psalm 103:8

SIT IN THAT TRUTH
LOVED BEYOND MEASURE

Take a few moments to ask God to remove any distractions and to silence your own voice and the enemy's voice, so that you can hear God clearly and focus on Him. Invite the Holy Spirit to help you as you work through these questions.

1. Do you truly believe that God loves you just as much today as He did before your marriage ended? Why or why not?

2. When you think about God's love, do you see it as something you can lose based on your choices, or something that remains steady no matter what? What has shaped that belief?

3. In what ways have you felt distant from God since your divorce? Do you believe that distance is coming from Him or from you?

4. When guilt or shame shows up, what are the specific thoughts or lies you hear about how God sees you?

5. Write the lies down. Then, find a Scripture that speaks truth against each one and write it out.

6. If nothing can separate you from God's love, what would it look like for you to live like that is true?

Chapter 3

The God Who Stays Close

Psalm 34:18

His presence sustains you in your brokenness. "The Lord is close to the brokenhearted; He rescues those whose spirits are crushed." (Psalm 34:18 NLT)

When your world falls apart, people scatter. Some don't know what to say. Others choose sides. Some quietly fade from your life because your brokenness makes them uncomfortable. And if you've felt that loss, I see you.

But here's the truth: God doesn't pull away from brokenness; He draws near to it.

Psalm 34:18 isn't just poetry; it's a promise. When your heart feels like it's in pieces, He leans closer towards you. When your spirit feels crushed under the weight of grief, confusion, or regret, He doesn't wait for you to stand back up before He comes to your side.

Jesus never avoided the hurting. He touched lepers (Mark 1:40-42). He wept with Mary and Martha (John 11:35). He restored Peter after the biggest failure of his life (John 21:15-17). Our God doesn't need you to be "put together" to be present with you.

And here's something you need to know: closeness to God isn't always about feeling goosebumps or hearing Him audibly speak. Sometimes His closeness shows up in the steady peace that makes no sense in the middle of chaos (Philippians 4:7). Sometimes it's the strength to take one more step when you think you are done. Sometimes it's the right verse at the right time, reminding you you're not forgotten.

The enemy will try to convince you that your brokenness makes you unworthy of God's presence. But the Word tells us the opposite: your brokenness is exactly what draws Him close.

So don't run from Him in this season. Run toward Him. Crawl if you must. Whisper if your voice can't carry. Because He's already right here.

Let's Pray Together

Father,

Thank You that You do not pull away from me in my brokenness, but instead You draw near to me. When I feel alone, remind me that You are present, even when I don't feel it. Help me to stop running from You and begin turning toward You, even if it's just one small step at a time. Where I've believed lies that I am too broken or too far gone, replace them with the truth that You are close. Give me peace in the middle of what doesn't make sense, and strength for today. Teach me to trust that You are here.

In Jesus' name,

Amen.

Sit With These Scriptures

"The Lord is close to the brokenhearted; He rescues those whose spirits are crushed." Psalm 34:18

"And the peace of God, which surpasses all understanding, will guard your hearts and your minds in Christ Jesus." Philippians 4:7

SIT IN THAT TRUTH
THE GOD WHO STAYS CLOSE

Take a few moments to ask God to remove any distractions and to silence your own voice and the enemy's voice, so that you can hear God clearly and focus on Him. Invite the Holy Spirit to help you as you work through these questions.

1. Think back to a moment in this season where you felt completely alone. What did that moment feel like, and what made it so heavy?

2. In that moment, where do you believe God was? Do you feel like He was absent, distant, or present in a way you didn't recognize at the time?

3. When you experience pain or brokenness, is your natural response to move toward God or pull away from Him? Why?

4. What lies have you believed about your brokenness, making you unworthy of God's presence?

5. If God is truly close to the brokenhearted, what would it look like for you to run toward Him in this season instead of away?

HARD TRUTH #2
MARRIAGE IS PART OF GOD'S DESIGN, BUT IT'S NOT A GUARANTEE

God created marriage; it was His idea. But while it's part of His design, it's not promised to everyone, and there's no guarantee that every marriage will last. Sometimes, despite our best intentions, our spouse or we make choices that move us away from God's best. In this section, we're going to talk about what happens when marriage doesn't go the way we planned, the role our choices play, and how God can redeem the story even when the marriage wasn't His perfect plan.

Chapter 4

God's Design For Covenant

Genesis 2:24

From the very beginning, God intended marriage to be the blueprint for humanity. "This explains why a man leaves his father and mother and is joined to his wife, and the two are united into one" (Genesis 2:24 NLT). Paul even reminds us that marriage reflects the mystery of Christ and the church (Ephesians 5:31-32).

But here's the hard truth: while marriage is part of His design, it's not a promise that everyone will experience, and it's not a guarantee that every marriage will last.

Somewhere along the way, we started treating marriage like the ultimate life achievement, as if you're married, you've "made it," and if you're not, you're somehow incomplete. But the Bible never says that. The ultimate prize is Jesus, not a spouse.

The reality is, not every marriage is chosen in prayer, led by the Spirit, or built on God's wisdom. Sometimes we enter relationships out of loneliness, fear, or cultural pressure. Sometimes we ignore the red flags because we're convinced love will fix them. And sometimes, even when we start well, sin, pride, and brokenness creep in and tear apart what we thought would stand forever.

This doesn't mean God can't or won't redeem a marriage; He absolutely can. I've seen Him do it. But He can also redeem you outside of that marriage. Sometimes His redemption happens within the covenant; other times, it happens in the healing that follows when the covenant is broken.

And while divorce was never His original design, He still works all things together for the good of those who love Him (Romans 8:28). Even this.

So, if your marriage ended, it doesn't mean you missed God's plan forever. It means you're in the middle of a chapter that God can still use, for your good, for His glory, and for your growth.

Let's Pray Together

Father,

Thank You for being a God of design and purpose, even when my story hasn't gone the way I expected. Where I have placed my worth in marriage or in my past, help me release that and see myself through Your eyes. Remind me that I have not missed Your plan, and that You are still working in every part of my story. Give me clarity where I need it, healing where I've been hurt, and trust to believe that You are not finished with me. Anchor me in Your truth, not in what I've lost. And teach me to walk forward in confidence, knowing You are still leading me.

In Jesus' name,

Amen.

Sit With These Scriptures

"This explains why a man leaves his father and mother and is joined to his wife, and the two are united into one." Genesis 2:24

"And we know that in all things God works for the good of those who love Him, who have been called according to His purpose." Romans 8:28

SIT IN THAT TRUTH
GOD'S DESIGN FOR COVENANT

Take a few moments to ask God to remove any distractions and to silence your own voice and the enemy's voice, so that you can hear God clearly and focus on Him. Invite the Holy Spirit to help you as you work through these questions.

1. Have you been holding marriage as the ultimate measure of your worth or God's favor? Be honest about where that belief may have taken root.

2 How has your view of marriage shaped the way you see yourself now that your marriage has ended?

3.Looking back, were there places where fear, loneliness, pressure, or ignoring red flags influenced your relationship decisions? What clarity do you have now?

4.Do you feel like your divorce means you've missed God's plan for your life, or do you believe He is still working in your story? Why?

5. If your identity is not found in your relationship status, what would it look like to begin seeing yourself through God's eyes instead?

Chapter 5

Free Will And Choice

Proverbs 15:22

The Book of Proverbs has a lot to say about the role that wisdom and counsel play in making life decisions. In fact, Proverbs 15:22 states, “Plans go wrong for lack of advice; but many advisers bring success.”

God’s design for marriage is perfect, but the people in it are not. He gave us free will, which means we can make wise, Spirit-led choices, or we can make decisions without Him and hope for the best. That rarely ends well.

Not every failed marriage is the result of a dramatic betrayal or a single moment that changed everything. Sometimes it is simply the outcome of a series of choices made without wisdom. Maybe we did not pray before the wedding. Maybe we ignored godly counsel because we did not want to hear it. And maybe we have asked for advice only from people who would tell us what we wanted to hear.

Proverbs 15:22 reminds us that God places wisdom around us for our protection. Counsel is not control. It is love. When we reject it, we often do not see the consequences until much later.

For some of us, divorce is the consequence of choices we can now see clearly in hindsight. That does not mean you are condemned. It means you are honest. There is a difference. God allows consequences, but He does not use them to define us. Conviction is meant to lead us to freedom, not trap us in shame. Romans 8:1 still stands. There is no condemnation for those who belong to Christ Jesus.

And here is something important. Just because divorce may be the consequence of a past choice does not mean staying in a destructive pattern would be obedience. God does not ask us to remain in places that are actively destroying us in order to prove our faithfulness. Sometimes the consequence of poor choices is the ending of a marriage, and even there, God meets us with mercy, truth, and freedom.

Freedom does not erase responsibility. It redeems it. God's grace does not excuse our choices, but it does meet us in their aftermath. He invites us to learn, to grow, and to choose differently going forward. Not from fear, but from wisdom. Not from shame, but from transformation.

Let's Pray Together

Father,

Thank You for meeting me with truth and grace. Give me the courage to look honestly at my past without falling into shame. Where I ignored wisdom or chose my own way, please bring clarity, not to condemn me, but to grow me. Help me to receive conviction as a gift that leads me to freedom. Teach me to seek wisdom, to listen to counsel, and to choose differently moving forward. Help me to remember and remind me often that my past does not define me. You do.

In Jesus' name,

Amen

Sit With These Scriptures

"Plans go wrong for lack of advice; many advisers bring success." Proverbs 15:22

"There is therefore now no condemnation for those who belong to Christ Jesus." Romans 8:1

SIT IN THAT TRUTH
FREE WILL AND CHOICE

Take a few moments to ask God to remove any distractions and to silence your own voice and the enemy's voice, so that you can hear God clearly and focus on Him. Invite the Holy Spirit to help you as you work through these questions.

1. Am I willing to look honestly at my past choices without letting them define me? What makes that difficult?

2.Looking back, where can I now see that I ignored wisdom, avoided counsel, or chose what I wanted over what was right?

3.How have I viewed counsel in the past—as protection or as restriction? What shaped that perspective?

4.When I think about the consequences of my choices, do I tend to move toward conviction that leads to growth, or toward shame that keeps me stuck?

5.What is one area where God is inviting me to choose differently going forward—not from fear, but from wisdom?

Chapter 6

Redeeming The Story

Romans 8:28

God works for good even when the marriage was not His perfect plan. We can find comfort in this verse, "And we know that God causes everything to work together for the good of those who love God and are called according to His purpose." (Romans 8:28 NLT)

Some of us look back and wonder if our marriage was ever part of God's perfect plan. Maybe we didn't ask Him. Maybe we ignored His nudges. Umm, remember those pesky red flags? Me too! Me too! Maybe we just didn't understand what a covenant meant at the time.

Here's the hope you need to hold onto, even if your marriage wasn't God's best for you, He can still redeem your story. Romans 8:28 doesn't say everything that happens is good. It says God works in everything for good. That includes the heartbreak, the mess, and the choices we wish we could undo. Our faith in God does not water down the pain; it is what sustains us in and through the fire of it all.

He can take the lessons learned, the compassion gained, and even the scars, and use them to shape you into someone stronger, wiser, and closer to Him. Redemption doesn't always mean restoring the marriage; sometimes it's restoring you. Sometimes it's walking forward so healed and free that the enemy regrets he ever messed with you.

Your marriage may have been one chapter, but it's not your whole book. God's not done writing, and His plot twists are always worth sticking around for.

Let's Pray Together

Father,

Thank You that nothing in my story is wasted in Your hands. Even the parts I don't understand, You are still working things out for good. Where I feel regret, pain, or confusion, remind me that You are not finished with me. Help me to trust that You can redeem what feels broken and use it for something greater. Give me hope for what's ahead and peace with what's behind. Teach me to see my story through Your eyes and to believe that You are still writing something beautiful.

In Jesus' name,

Amen.

Sit With These Scriptures

"And we know that God causes everything to work together for the good of those who love God and are called according to His purpose."Romans 8:28

"He heals the brokenhearted and bandages their wounds. "Psalm 147:3

SIT IN THAT TRUTH
REDEEMING THE STORY

Take a few moments to ask God to remove any distractions and to silence your own voice and the enemy's voice, so that you can hear God clearly and focus on Him. Invite the Holy Spirit to help you as you work through these questions.

1.When you look back on your marriage, do you struggle with wondering if it was outside of God's plan? What thoughts come up for you?

2.What are some lessons, growth, or clarity you've gained through your marriage or divorce that you wouldn't have had otherwise?

3. Is there a part of your story that you still feel is too broken, too messy, or too far gone for God to redeem? What is it?

4. When you hear that God works all things together for good, do you believe that includes your story, or do you feel like yours is the exception? Why?

5. If God is still writing your story, what would it look like to trust Him with what comes next, even if you don't fully understand it yet?

HARD TRUTH #3 REDEMPTION CAN HAPPEN INSIDE OR OUTSIDE THE MARRIAGE

When we hear the word redemption, many of us picture a broken marriage being put back together. And yes, sometimes God does that. But if you're holding this book, your story has already taken a different turn. The papers are signed, the marriage is over, and yet, God's redemptive power is still fully at work in your life.

Redemption isn't limited to getting back what was lost; sometimes it's about gaining something entirely new. God can heal wounds, restore joy, and rebuild your sense of worth without putting you back in the same relationship. In this section, we'll look at how He brings restoration to our hearts, beauty from the ashes, and ongoing transformation that continues long after the divorce.

Chapter 7

Restored From The Inside Out

Psalm 147:3

God's restoration does not begin with fixing circumstances. It begins with healing hearts.

When a marriage ends, the most damage often occurs internally. Trust is broken. Identity feels shaken. Hope can feel fragile or out of reach. And while people may pressure you to "move on" or "get over it," God does something very different. He slows down. He draws near. He tends to our wounds, the ones that cannot be seen.

Psalm 147:3 reminds us that God is not distant from brokenness. He is close to it. He heals the brokenhearted and binds up their wounds. That means He does not rush you. He does not minimize your pain. He does not demand quick fixes or shallow faith.

Restoration is not about going back to what was. It is about being made whole where you were once fractured. God knows how to restore your sense of worth, your ability to trust again, and your confidence in who you are in Him. He knows how to heal places that were slowly worn down over time.

You may never return to your former spouse, and that does not mean restoration failed. Sometimes restoration looks like peace where there was chaos, clarity where there was confusion, and strength where there was once fear.

God's restoration is personal. It is intentional. And it does not require you to stay in harm's way to prove your faithfulness.

Let's Pray Together

Father,

You see every hidden place in my heart, every wound I've tried to ignore, rush past, or carry on my own. Thank You that You are not distant from my pain, but near to it. Gentle with it. Intentional with it. Teach me to slow down and let You do the deep work in me. Heal the places where my trust was broken, where my identity was shaken, and where my hope feels fragile. Restore what has been worn down, not just on the outside, but within me. Help me not to rush healing or settle for surface-level peace. Give me the courage to invite You into the hard places and the patience to trust Your timing. Make me whole again, not by returning me to what was, but by leading me into who You are calling me to be.

In Jesus' name,

Amen.

Sit With These Scriptures

"He heals the brokenhearted and binds up their wounds." Psalm 147:3

"The Lord is near to the brokenhearted and saves the crushed in spirit." Psalm 34:18

SIT IN THAT TRUTH
RESTORED FROM THE INSIDE OUT

Take a few moments to ask God to remove any distractions and to silence your own voice and the enemy's voice, so that you can hear God clearly and focus on Him. Invite the Holy Spirit to help you as you work through these questions.

1.What part of your heart still feels wounded, guarded, or not fully healed from your marriage or divorce?

2.Have you felt pressure from others, or even yourself, to "move on" before you were truly healed? What has that looked like?

3. Do you believe God cares about your emotional healing, or do you tend to focus more on changing your circumstances? Why?

4. In what ways has your identity, trust, or sense of worth been affected, and where do you need God to restore you from the inside out?

5. What would it look like to let God heal you slowly and fully, rather than rushing the process or numbing the pain?

Chapter 8

Healing After It Ends

Isaiah 61:3

"To all who mourn, He will give a crown of beauty for ashes, a joyous blessing instead of mourning, festive praise instead of despair. In their righteousness, they will be like great oaks that the LORD has planted for his own glory." (Isaiah 61:3 NLT)

Divorce leaves ashes.

Ashes of dreams you thought would last forever.

Ashes of plans you built around someone else.

Ashes of the version of you that existed in that marriage.

But Isaiah 61:3 is God's promise that ashes aren't the end of your story. Where you see loss, He sees a blank canvas. Where you see rubble, He sees raw material for a new foundation. He doesn't just sweep the ashes away; He transforms them into something beautiful that reflects His glory.

Here's the thing: healing is not instant. You can't rush it, skip it, or fake it. But you can position yourself to receive it. Healing starts with honesty before God, telling Him where it hurts, where you're angry, where you're ashamed. And then it's about letting Him replace those things with joy, praise, and peace that doesn't make sense to the world (Philippians 4:7).

Your marriage may be over, but your life is not on pause. You can dream again. You can laugh again. You can live fully again, not because the pain disappears, but because God has a way of weaving joy into even the deepest wounds.

Remember: ashes are what's left after the fire. But in the hands of the Creator, ashes are the soil for something new to grow.

Let's Pray Together

Father,

You see the ashes in my life, the places where things didn't turn out the way I hoped, the loss, the grief, and the parts of me that still feel broken. Thank You that You don't waste any of it. Thank You that You are a God who restores, redeems, and rebuilds. Teach me to bring every part of my heart before You honestly, without hiding, without rushing, without pretending. Meet me in my grief and begin to replace what feels heavy with Your peace, Your joy, and Your presence. Help me trust that You are already working, even when I can't see it. Give me faith to believe that beauty is coming, that joy will return, and that my story is still being written by Your hands. Take these ashes and make something beautiful for Your glory.

In Jesus' name,

Amen.

Sit With These Scriptures

"To all who mourn, He will give a crown of beauty for ashes, a joyous blessing instead of mourning, festive praise instead of despair." Isaiah 61:3

"And the peace of God, which surpasses all understanding, will guard your hearts and your minds in Christ Jesus." Philippians 4:7

SIT IN THAT TRUTH
HEALING AFTER IT ENDS

Take a few moments to ask God to remove any distractions and to silence your own voice and the enemy's voice, so that you can hear God clearly and focus on Him. Invite the Holy Spirit to help you as you work through these questions.

1.What "ashes" are you currently holding onto from your marriage or divorce? Be honest about what still feels lost or broken.

2.Is there an area of your life where you're struggling to believe God can bring beauty from what feels ruined? What is it?

3.Have you been trying to rush your healing, avoid it, or pretend you're further along than you are? What would honesty with God look like right now?

4.What emotions are hardest for you to bring before God, anger, grief, shame, disappointment? Why do you think that is?

5.If God truly brings beauty from ashes, what would it look like to begin thanking Him in advance, even before you see the outcome?

Chapter 9

God's Ongoing Work

Philippians 1:6

He is not finished with you yet. In fact, according to this verse in Philippians, God will continue to work on you until His work is complete in you.

"And I am certain that God, who began the good work within you, will continue His work until it is finally finished." (Philippians 1:6 NLT)

Divorce can make you feel like you're starting over from scratch, like all the work God was doing in your life before just got bulldozed. But our verse for today says otherwise. God finishes what He starts. He doesn't abandon you in the middle of the rebuild.

The truth is that healing and growth are rarely neat and tidy. Some days you'll feel strong, and other days it will take everything in you just to get out of bed. Some days you'll feel free, and other days you'll have to fight off the "what if" thoughts that creep in. That's not failure, that's process.

And in that process, God is still working. Even when you can't see progress, He's laying new foundations:

- Restoring your identity in Him (1 Peter 2:9)
- Rebuilding your ability to trust (Psalm 28:7)
- Renewing your mind to think according to His truth

instead of the lies of the enemy (Romans 12:2)

He's also preparing you for the next chapters of your life, ones you might not even be able to imagine right now. That's what makes this verse so powerful: God has no unfinished projects. If He started something in you before the divorce, He's still at it.

So, give yourself permission to be "in process." God's timeline is perfect, and He's not letting go of you until the work is done.

Let's Pray Together

Father,

Thank You that You are not finished with me. Even when I feel stuck, discouraged, or unsure of where I'm going, You are still working. Remind me that I am not abandoned in the middle of the process. That every step, even the slow and messy ones, is part of what You are doing in me. Help me to trust Your timing when I want things to move faster. Give me grace for the days that feel heavy and faith for the days I can't see progress. Strengthen me to keep showing up, to keep healing, and to keep believing that You are building something new in my life. Thank You that You finish what You start. And thank You that I am still in Your hands.

In Jesus' name,

Amen

Sit With These Scriptures

"And I am certain that God, who began the good work within you, will continue His work until it is finally finished." Philippians 1:6

"Behold, I am doing a new thing; now it springs forth, do you not perceive it?" Isaiah 43:19

SIT IN THAT TRUTH
GOD'S ONGOING WORK

Take a few moments to ask God to remove any distractions and to silence your own voice and the enemy's voice, so that you can hear God clearly and focus on Him. Invite the Holy Spirit to help you as you work through these questions.

1.In what ways have you felt like your life has been "reset" or undone after your divorce?

2.Do you struggle to believe that God is still actively working in your life right now? Why or why not?

3.Where do you see evidence, even small, that God is rebuilding or restoring something within you?

4.How do you typically respond on the hard days when healing feels slow or progress feels invisible?

5.What would it look like to fully embrace being “in process” instead of expecting yourself to have it all together?

HARD TRUTH #4
DIVORCE WILL CHANGE YOU, BUT IT DOES NOT DEFINE YOU

Divorce will change you; there's no way around it. You won't come out the same as you went in. You'll think differently, you'll see life differently, and sometimes, you'll even see yourself differently. But here's the thing: it doesn't get to define you. Yes, this is part of your story. But it's not the title of your story. It's one chapter in a book God is still writing. And He's the kind of Author who knows how to use even the painful chapters to set up an incredible plot twist.

In this section, we're going to talk about who you really are. Not the identity the divorce tried to give you, but the identity God already gave you before the foundation of the world. In this section, we're digging deeper into what it means to live as a new creation, walking out your identity in Christ, and stepping boldly into the new life He's calling you to.

Chapter 10

A New Creation

2 Corinthians 5:17

You are not your past. The Bible says that, "anyone who belongs to Christ has become a new person. The old life is gone; a new life has begun!" (2 Corinthians 5:17 NLT)

Let's be honest, divorce can leave you feeling like you've been wrecked beyond repair. It can convince you that you're "damaged goods" or that the best version of your life is over. But God's Word says something entirely different: if you belong to Christ, you are a new creation. Not "kind of improved." Not "patched up just enough to get by." New. Brand new.

When Paul wrote this in 2 Corinthians 5:17, he was talking to people who had real baggage, and his point was clear: your past, no matter how messy, doesn't have the power to define your future when you're in Christ. That includes the life you lived before the divorce and the life that resulted from it. Here's the thing: stepping into this "new creation" life is both an instant reality and a process. God declares you new the moment you put your faith in Him, but He also walks you through the journey of learning to live like it. That means some days you'll feel brand new, and other days, you'll feel like the old you is still hanging around. That's okay. The process is proof that He's still working on you.

Let's Pray Together

Father,

Thank You that my past does not define me. Thank You that in You, I am made new, not patched up, not barely holding it together, but truly transformed. Help me to release every label that does not come from You. Where I have believed lies about my worth, my identity, or my future, replace them with Your truth. Teach me how to live as the new creation You say I already am. Even on the days it feels hard or unfamiliar, remind me that You are still shaping me, still renewing me, and still calling me forward. Give me the courage to walk in my new identity and the confidence to believe that my best is not behind me, but ahead of me in You.

In Jesus' name,

Amen.

Sit With These Scriptures

"This means that anyone who belongs to Christ has become a new person. The old life is gone; a new life has begun!" 2 Corinthians 5:17

"For we are His workmanship, created in Christ Jesus for good works, which God prepared beforehand, that we should walk in them." Ephesians 2:10

SIT IN THAT TRUTH
A NEW CREATION

Take a few moments to ask God to remove any distractions and to silence your own voice and the enemy's voice, so that you can hear God clearly and focus on Him. Invite the Holy Spirit to help you as you work through these questions.

1.What labels or identities have you silently carried since your divorce (damaged, rejected, not enough, too much)?

2.Which of those feel the hardest to let go of, and why?

3. Do you truly believe you are a "new creation," or do you feel like a repaired version of your old self? Be honest.

4. What lies about your worth or future tend to resurface when you're tired, triggered, or discouraged?

5. What would it look like to start agreeing with God about who you are, even when your feelings don't match yet?

Chapter 11

Identity In Christ

1 Peter 2:9

You are chosen and set apart. The word of God says, "But you are not like that, for you are a chosen people. You are royal priests, a holy nation, God's very own possession." (1 Peter 2:9 NLT)

If divorce has a "side effect" no one talks about, it's the identity crisis it can trigger. You go from being someone's spouse to... what? Single? Co-parent? Ex-wife or ex-husband? The world loves labels, and if you're not careful, you'll start wearing one that was never yours to begin with.

God's Word tells a different story. In 1 Peter 2:9, He calls you chosen. Not "left over." Not "second best." Chosen. He says you are His very own possession; treasured, wanted, and set apart for His purposes.

This means your worth didn't take a hit when your marriage ended. Your value isn't determined by your relationship status. You're not "less than" because you're divorced, and you're not "more than" when you're married. Your identity is fixed in Christ, and nothing, not even the most painful chapter of your life, can change that.

And when you start living from that truth, everything shifts. Your decisions, your boundaries, your relationships, even how you talk to yourself in the mirror, all start to reflect the reality of who God says you are.

Let's Pray Together

Father,

Thank You for choosing me. Not because of my past, my performance, or my circumstances, but because of Your love. Help me to let go of every label that does not come from You. Where I've believed I am less than, forgotten, or defined by what I've been through, remind me of who I truly am in You. Teach me to live from my identity, not for it. Strengthen me to walk confidently in You, as someone who is chosen, set apart, and deeply loved by You. Let that truth shape how I see myself, how I make decisions, and how I show up in the world.

In Jesus' name,

Amen.

Sit With These Scriptures

"But you are a chosen race, a royal priesthood, a holy nation, a people for His own possession..." 1 Peter 2:9

"See what kind of love the Father has given to us, that we should be called children of God; and so we are." 1 John 3:1

SIT IN THAT TRUTH
IDENTITY IN CHRIST

Take a few moments to ask God to remove any distractions and to silence your own voice and the enemy's voice, so that you can hear God clearly and focus on Him. Invite the Holy Spirit to help you as you work through these questions.

1.What labels have you taken on since your divorce that don't align with how God sees you?

2.Which identity feels louder in your life right now, what you've been called by people or what God calls you? Why?

3. Do you struggle to believe that you are chosen, wanted, and set apart by God? What makes that hard to receive?

4. How has your relationship status shaped the way you see your worth or value?

5. What would change in your life if you truly lived from the identity God has already given you?

Chapter 12

Stepping Into New Life

Isaiah 43:18-19

Forget the former things, and see the new. The Lord is a master at making a person new and bringing them into something new as well. Isaiah states, "But forget all that, it is nothing compared to what I am going to do. For I am about to do something new." (Isaiah 43:18-19 NLT)

Here's something I've learned: you can't step fully into the new life God has for you while clinging to the wreckage of the old one. That doesn't mean you erase the past; it means you stop letting it steer the ship.

Isaiah 43:18-19 isn't just a nice verse for a coffee mug. God was telling His people, who had been through loss, exile, and hardship, that He was doing something so new and unexpected that the past paled in comparison.

That's the kind of God you serve. He's not just in the business of patching up the old. He's in the business of creating something entirely new. And yes, that includes your life after divorce.

But here's the challenge: new requires space. If your hands are full of old memories, bitterness, or regret, there's no room for what He's trying to give you.

So, what's the thing you need to set down so you can take hold of the new? A toxic narrative about yourself, a deep hurt you haven't let go of, or perhaps a dream you've been scared to dream again. Whatever it is, today's the day to start loosening your grip.

Let's Pray Together

Father,

Thank You for always doing something new. Even when I can't see it yet, even when I'm still holding onto pieces of the past, You are moving. Help me to release what I've been gripping too tightly. The hurt, the regret, the old narratives, and the things that no longer serve what You are doing in my life. Give me the courage to let go and the faith to trust what You are placing before me. Open my eyes to see the new thing You are already preparing and soften my heart to receive it. Teach me to walk forward without being anchored to what's behind me. To live with open hands, ready for whatever You have next.

In Jesus' name,

Amen.

Sit With These Scriptures

"Remember not the former things, nor consider the things of old. Behold, I am doing a new thing..." Isaiah 43:18–19

"Therefore, if anyone is in Christ, he is a new creation. The old has passed away; behold, the new has come." 2 Corinthians 5:17

SIT IN THAT TRUTH
STEPPING INTO NEW LIFE

Take a few moments to ask God to remove any distractions and to silence your own voice and the enemy's voice, so that you can hear God clearly and focus on Him. Invite the Holy Spirit to help you as you work through these questions.

1. What part of your past are you still holding onto that may be keeping you from fully stepping into what God is doing now?

2. Is there a story, memory, or identity from your divorce that you keep replaying? How is it shaping your present?

3. What feels hardest to release right now, bitterness, regret, fear, or control? Why?

4. Do you believe God is truly doing something new in your life, or does it feel easier to stay focused on what was?

5. What would it look like to create space in your life, emotionally, mentally, and spiritually, for the new thing God is bringing?

HARD TRUTH #5
YOU WILL FACE JUDGMENT FROM PEOPLE

Let's just call it like it is, people talk. They speculate. They fill in the blanks with their own assumptions, and they don't always get it right. And unfortunately, some of the loudest voices can come from the people who never sat in your marriage for a single day.

Some will decide you were wrong before they even ask your side of the story. Some will assume that because you're divorced, you must have "missed God's plan." Others will treat you like a spiritual project that needs "fixing" as if you're somehow a lesser Christian now.

I wish I could tell you that following Jesus would shield you from that. But the truth is, Jesus Himself faced constant criticism, unfair judgment, and complete misunderstanding. And if the world didn't give Him the benefit of the doubt, it's not going to give it to you either (John 15:18).

The comfort is this: He gets it. He understands what it's like to be misrepresented. And He's already given us the blueprint for standing in truth and grace when people get it wrong. In this section, we will learn how to handle being misunderstood, respond like Christ, and understand God as our defender.

Chapter 13

Jesus Understands Being Misunderstood

John 15: 18-19

If the world hated Him then the world is going to misunderstand you and sometimes hate you as well. Jesus said it this way, "If the world hates you, remember that it hated me first." (John 15:18 NLT)

There's something strangely freeing about realizing Jesus walked this road before you. He was criticized for healing on the Sabbath, judged for eating with "the wrong people," accused of blasphemy, and misunderstood by His own family.

If you've ever felt like no one sees the full picture, like you're living under a cloud of other people's assumptions, you're in good company. Jesus knows the sting of being judged without a fair hearing. And that's why He doesn't just sympathize with you; He stands with you in it.

Here's the thing: when you know God sees the truth, you can stop exhausting yourself trying to convince everyone else. That's not your assignment. Your job is to walk in obedience to Him, not to manage public opinion.

And let me just be your friend for a second, some people want to misunderstand you. Not everyone is interested in truth; some are more comfortable with their version of the story. Chasing their approval is like trying to catch smoke.

Instead, keep your focus where it belongs, on the One who knows every detail and still calls you loved, chosen, and redeemed. He's the only one qualified to define you.

Let's Pray Together

Father,

Thank You that You see what others don't. You know the full story, the parts that were hidden, the motives, the pain, and the truth behind it all. When I feel misunderstood or judged, remind me that I am not alone in this. Jesus, You walked this road, and You understand what it feels like to be misrepresented. Help me to release the need to explain myself to everyone. Give me peace in knowing that Your opinion of me is what matters most. Teach me to walk in obedience, not in fear of what others think. And where I feel the weight of judgment, remind me that You are my defender.

In Jesus' name,

Amen.

Sit With These Scriptures

"If the world hates you, remember that it hated me first." John 15:18

"The Lord will fight for you; you need only to be still." Exodus 14:14

SIT IN THAT TRUTH
JESUS UNDERSTANDS BEING MISUNDERSTOOD

Take a few moments to ask God to remove any distractions and to silence your own voice and the enemy's voice, so that you can hear God clearly and focus on Him. Invite the Holy Spirit to help you as you work through these questions.

1. Where in your life do you feel most misunderstood right now?

2. Are there people whose opinions you're still trying to change or manage? Who are they?

3. How has the fear of being misunderstood or judged affected your decisions, your voice, or your confidence?

4. Do you truly believe that God seeing and knowing the full truth is enough, or do you still feel the need to be validated by others? Why?

5. What would it look like to release the need to be understood by everyone and instead focus on obedience to God?

Chapter 14

Responding Like Christ

1 Peter 2:23

Jesus did not retaliate, in fact the Bible says, "He did not retaliate when he was insulted, nor threaten revenge when he suffered. He left his case in the hands of God, who always judges fairly." (1 Peter 2:23 NLT)

If anyone had the right to fight back, it was Jesus. He could have silenced His accusers with a single word, and that word could have knocked them flat. But He didn't. He stayed quiet, not because He was weak, but because He trusted His Father to handle it.

That's hard for us, right? We live in a world where the instinct is to defend ourselves, to post the screenshots, to "set the record straight" so people will know the truth. But here's the thing: your healing can't live in the same room as your obsession with vindication. You can't keep looking over your shoulder at what people think and expect to move forward at the same time.

When you choose to respond like Christ, you're not letting people "get away with it." You're letting God take the case, and Scripture says He judges fairly every single time. His justice is perfect. Yours? Well... let's just say ours is usually laced with a little pride and payback.

I'm not saying it's easy. It will take every ounce of self-control you have and then some. But the reward is peace. Peace from not having to rehearse the argument in your head. Peace from not having to check if they "liked" your post. Peace from letting go of proving yourself.

Let's Pray Together

Father,

You see every situation where I've been misunderstood, misrepresented, or hurt. And You know how much I want to defend myself and make things right. But today, I choose to trust You. I choose to place this situation in Your hands, knowing that You judge fairly and completely. Help me to let go of the need to prove myself. Give me the strength to respond with grace instead of reacting out of emotion. Guard my heart from bitterness, pride, and the desire for revenge. And replace it with Your peace, the kind that comes from trusting You fully. Remind me that I don't have to fight every battle, because You are fighting for me.

In Jesus' name,

Amen.

Sit With These Scriptures

"He did not retaliate when he was insulted... He left his case in the hands of God, who always judges fairly." 1 Peter 2:23

"Do not take revenge, my dear friends, but leave room for God's wrath..." Romans 12:19

SIT IN THAT TRUTH
RESPONDING LIKE JESUS

Take a few moments to ask God to remove any distractions and to silence your own voice and the enemy's voice, so that you can hear God clearly and focus on Him. Invite the Holy Spirit to help you as you work through these questions.

1. Where have you felt the strongest urge to defend yourself or "set the record straight"?

2. What emotions come up when you think about not responding: anger, fear, injustice, or frustration?

3. Do you trust God to handle the situation, or do you feel like it's your responsibility to make things right? Why?

4. How has the desire for vindication affected your peace or your ability to move forward?

5. What would it look like, practically, to release control and let God be your defender in this situation?

Chapter 15

God As Your Defender

Psalm 37:5-6

He will make your innocence shine. The psalmist puts it this way, "Commit everything you do to the Lord. Trust him, and he will help you. He will make your innocence radiate like the dawn, and the justice of your cause will shine like the noonday sun." (Psalm 37:5-6 NLT)

Let's get real: some people will never change their opinion of you. And honestly? That's fine. God's not asking you to chase down every rumor or justify every decision you've made.

When you commit your life to the Lord, not just the good, polished parts, but the messy, painful, and misunderstood parts, you're telling Him, "This is Yours now." And He takes that seriously. He steps in as your advocate, your defender, your witness.

David wrote these words while he was being hunted, lied about, and betrayed by people he had once trusted. Yet he believed God would make the truth shine so brightly that no one could deny it. That's the kind of quiet confidence you can walk in as well.

Here's the best part: when God is your defender, you don't have to fight every battle. You can spend your energy on healing, building, and living in the purpose He still has for you. You can hold your head high knowing the One who matters most already knows your innocence.

Let's Pray Together

Father,

Thank You that I don't have to defend myself in every situation. You see the truth, and You care about what I've walked through. Help me to release the need to control how others perceive me. Teach me to trust You with every part of my story, even the parts that feel misunderstood. When I'm tempted to step in and fight for myself, remind me that You are my defender. That You are working on my behalf, even when I can't see it yet. Give me peace in Your timing and confidence in Your justice. And help me to focus my energy on healing, growing, and walking in the purpose You have for me. Thank You that my life is safe in Your hands.

In Jesus' name,

Amen.

Sit With These Scriptures

"Commit your way to the Lord; trust in Him, and He will act." Psalm 37:5–6

"The Lord is my light and my salvation; whom shall I fear? The Lord is the stronghold of my life..." Psalm 27:1

SIT IN THAT TRUTH
GOD AS YOUR DEFENDER

Take a few moments to ask God to remove any distractions and to silence your own voice and the enemy's voice, so that you can hear God clearly and focus on Him. Invite the Holy Spirit to help you as you work through these questions.

1. Where in your life are you still trying to defend yourself or control how others see you?

2. What would it look like to truly "commit everything" to God, even the parts of your story that feel misunderstood?

3. Do you trust God to bring truth to light in His timing, or do you feel pressure to make it happen yourself? Why?

4. How would your thoughts, emotions, or actions change if you fully believed God is your defender?

5. What is one situation you can intentionally release to God today instead of carrying it on your own?

HARD TRUTH #6
YOUR HEART WILL NEED HEALING TOO

Here's a truth that's easy to overlook, even if your ex was 90% of the problem. And let's be real, it takes two to win, and it takes two to fail. Even if that 90% were true, you're still carrying wounds that need tending. Divorce isn't just a legal process; it's a ripping apart of something that was meant to be whole. And whether you left, they left, or you both agreed to walk away, the tearing still leaves scars.

Sometimes we get so caught up in the details of what they did wrong that we skip over the healing our own hearts need. But here's the thing, God isn't just interested in fixing "what happened." He's after you. Your wholeness. Your restoration. Your freedom.

Healing starts when we stop rushing past the pain and let God search the places we'd rather ignore. It's not about shame; it's about surgery. In this section, we will learn how God wants to heal what's infected, mend what's torn, and make you stronger than before. But He won't force it; you must invite Him in.

Chapter 16

Search My Heart

Psalm 139:23-24

Inviting God to examine us isn't always easy but necessary. The word of the Lord says, "Search me, O God, and know my heart; test me and know my anxious thoughts. Point out anything in me that offends you and lead me along the path of everlasting life." (Psalm 139:23-24 NLT)

David's prayer here is both brave and risky. He's basically saying, "God, go ahead and shine a spotlight on my soul. Show me the stuff I don't even want to see." That takes courage, especially after divorce, when it's tempting to focus on all the ways we were wronged.

But this isn't about playing the blame game. It's about letting God reveal the places where bitterness, fear, or unhealthy patterns might be taking root. Because if we don't deal with those, they'll show up again in the next season. Whether that season is in new relationships, in our parenting, in our friendships, or in our walk with Him.

Let God search you, not so He can condemn you, but so He can heal you. The enemy would love for you to stay in self-protection mode forever, but God's goal is freedom, and freedom always starts with truth.

Let's Pray Together

Father,

I invite You into the places in my heart that I've been avoiding. The thoughts, the patterns, the wounds, and the areas I don't fully understand. Search me and know me completely. Not to condemn me, but to heal me. Give me the courage to face what You reveal. And the humility to surrender anything that is not aligned with You. Where I've built walls out of fear or self-protection, gently tear them down. And replace them with truth, freedom, and wholeness. Thank You that You are patient with me, kind in Your correction, and faithful to complete the work You've started in me.

In Jesus' name,

Amen.

Sit With These Scriptures

"Search me, O God, and know my heart... point out anything in me that offends You and lead me along the path of everlasting life." Psalm 139:23–24

"If we confess our sins, He is faithful and just to forgive us our sins and to cleanse us from all unrighteousness." 1 John 1:9

SIT IN THAT TRUTH
SEARCH MY HEART

Take a few moments to ask God to remove any distractions and to silence your own voice and the enemy's voice, so that you can hear God clearly and focus on Him. Invite the Holy Spirit to help you as you work through these questions.

1. When you ask God to search your heart, what feels most uncomfortable or risky about that?

2. Are there any patterns, reactions, or behaviors you've noticed in yourself that you haven't fully addressed yet?

3. Where might bitterness, fear, or self-protection still be taking root in your life?

4. Do you tend to avoid self-reflection because it feels like condemnation instead of healing? Why?

5. What would it look like to trust that God reveals things in your heart not to shame you, but to free you?

Chapter 17

Healing From Within

Ezekiel 36:26

You are promised a new heart and a new spirit. This promise is found in Ezekiel, which states, "And I will give you a new heart, and I will put a new spirit in you. I will take out your stony, stubborn heart and give you a tender, responsive heart." (Ezekiel 36:26 NLT)

God doesn't just want to slap a bandage on your wounds. He's in the business of transformation. That means He doesn't just make you better, He makes you new.

Think about that: a new heart. A tender heart. A responsive heart. One that's not hardened by betrayal or dulled by disappointment. One that beats in sync with His.

Sometimes after a painful marriage and a brutal divorce, it's easy to believe your heart will always be guarded, cold, or too broken to fully love again. But God has a track record of bringing life to dead places. If He can breathe life into dry bones as He did in Ezekiel 37, He can absolutely breathe life into you.

Healing from within doesn't happen overnight, but it does happen. The more you let Him in through prayer, His Word, and honest conversations with safe people, the more your heart softens, strengthens, and opens again. Yes, it takes time, but it's possible.

Let's Pray Together

Father,

Thank You that You don't leave my heart as it is. That You see every place that's been wounded, hardened, or shut down, and You are willing to make it new. I give You access to those places today. Even the ones I've tried to protect or avoid. Soften what has become hard. Heal what has been broken. And restore what feels lost within me. Help me to trust You with my heart again. To believe that I am not too far gone, too damaged, or too guarded for Your healing power. Make my heart tender, responsive, and aligned with Yours.

In Jesus' name,

Amen.

Sit With These Scriptures

"And I will give you a new heart, and I will put a new spirit in you..." Ezekiel 36:26

"He restores my soul. He leads me in paths of righteousness for His name's sake." Psalm 23:3

SIT IN THAT TRUTH
HEALING FROM WITHIN

Take a few moments to ask God to remove any distractions and to silence your own voice and the enemy's voice, so that you can hear God clearly and focus on Him. Invite the Holy Spirit to help you as you work through these questions.

1. In what ways has your heart become guarded, hardened, or hesitant after your divorce?

2. Do you find yourself believing that parts of your heart are too damaged to fully heal? Where did that belief come from?

3. What fears come up when you think about having a soft, open, and responsive heart again?

4. How have you been protecting your heart, and are those protections helping you heal or keeping you stuck?

5. What would it look like to trust God with your heart again, even in the vulnerable places?

Chapter 18

Walking In Wholeness

Proverbs 4:23

Walking in wholeness means that you guard your heart. Proverbs 4:23 says, "Guard your heart above all else, for it determines the course of your life."

Once God begins to heal your heart, your role shifts from wounded to watchful. Guarding your heart doesn't mean locking it in a vault and never trusting anyone again. It means using wisdom about what (and who) you allow to shape your thoughts, emotions, and actions.

Walking in wholeness means you're intentional about what you let in and what you keep out. You know the difference between healthy vulnerability and self-sabotage. You recognize the red flags you ignored before. You prioritize time with God because you know He's the source of your peace.

The truth is, guarding your heart is an ongoing process. The enemy will try to creep back in through old wounds, toxic relationships, or lies about your worth. But now you're not defenseless, you've got the armor of God (Ephesians 6), the wisdom of His Word, and the strength of the Holy Spirit inside you.

Let's Pray Together

Father,

Thank You for the healing You've begun in my heart. Thank You that

You don't just restore me, but You also teach me how to walk in wisdom moving forward. Help me to guard my heart in a way that honors You. Not out of fear, but out of discernment. Give me clarity to recognize what is healthy and what is not. Strength to set boundaries where needed, and wisdom to choose what I allow to shape my heart. Keep me grounded in Your truth so that I am not easily swayed by old patterns or lies. And help me to stay close to You, knowing You are the source of my peace, my strength, and my direction.

In Jesus' name,

Amen.

Sit With These Scriptures

"Guard your heart above all else, for it determines the course of your life." Proverbs 4:23

"Above all, put on love, which binds everything together in perfect harmony." Colossians 3:14

SIT IN THAT TRUTH
WALKING IN WHOLENESS

Take a few moments to ask God to remove any distractions and to silence your own voice and the enemy's voice, so that you can hear God clearly and focus on Him. Invite the Holy Spirit to help you as you work through these questions.

1. What areas of your life currently have the most influence over your heart (people, thoughts, habits, environments)?

2. Are there any relationships or patterns that you know are not healthy, but you've been hesitant to set boundaries around?

3. Do you guard your heart from a place of wisdom or a place of fear? How can you tell the difference in the way it shows up in your life?

4. What "red flags" do you recognize now that you may have ignored in the past?

5. What would it look like to actively guard your heart while still remaining open to what God wants to do in your life?

HARD TRUTH #7
FORGIVENESS IS REQUIRED, BUT RECONCILIATION IS NOT

Forgiveness is one of those words that sounds holy and noble until you have to actually do it. And when you've been betrayed, abandoned, or deeply hurt, it can feel downright impossible. But here's the hard truth: if you want to live free, you don't get to skip it.

Now, hear me: forgiveness is not the same as reconciliation. Forgiving someone doesn't mean you have to let them back into your inner circle, stay married while ignoring patterns of abandonment and/or abuse, or pretend as if nothing happened. Forgiveness is about releasing them from the debt they owe you so you can walk in freedom with God. Reconciliation requires repentance, change, and trust from both parties. And sometimes that never comes.

And sometimes, God Himself is the one who leads you out of a relationship. Not because He wants to see you in pain, but because He knows staying will destroy you. His heart for you is wholeness, not misery. In Proverbs 22:3, His Word tells us to forgive, yes, but also to be wise, to guard our hearts, and to walk away from danger when we see it. In this section, we will discover freedom in forgiveness and biblical boundaries.

Chapter 19

THE CALL TO FORGIVE

Colossians 3:13

Forgive as the Lord has forgiven you. As difficult as that may sound, the word of the Lord is clear, "Make allowance for each other's faults and forgive anyone who offends you. Remember, the Lord forgave you, so you must forgive others." (Colossians 3:13 NLT)

Let's be honest, forgiveness is rarely convenient. It's not like you wake up one morning, stretch, and say, "You know what? I think I'll let go of all my bitterness before breakfast." No, forgiveness is a choice you make, often repeatedly, because God has asked you to, and because you know what holding onto it will do to you.

Unforgiveness is like drinking poison and expecting the other person to die. It eats away at your peace, your joy, and your ability to hear from God. But when you forgive, you're not saying, "What happened was okay." You're saying, "I refuse to let what happened keep me in chains."

The standard for our forgiveness isn't the other person's apology; it's God's forgiveness toward us. And let's be real, He's forgiven us for more than we'd like to admit.

Let's Pray Together

Father,

You know how hard this is. You see the hurt, the betrayal, and the weight

I've been carrying. But You've also shown me what true forgiveness looks like. You forgave me fully, freely, and without hesitation. Today, I choose to forgive. Not because it's easy, and not because the other person deserves it, but because You've called me to it and I want to walk in freedom. Help me release what I've been holding onto. And when my feelings don't line up, remind me that forgiveness is a decision I can make daily. Heal my heart in the process and replace bitterness with peace.

In Jesus' name,

Amen.

Sit With These Scriptures

"Forgive as the Lord forgave you." Colossians 3:13

"Get rid of all bitterness, rage and anger... forgiving each other, just as in Christ God forgave you." Ephesians 4:31–32

SIT IN THAT TRUTH
THE CALL TO FORGIVE

Take a few moments to ask God to remove any distractions and to silence your own voice and the enemy's voice, so that you can hear God clearly and focus on Him. Invite the Holy Spirit to help you as you work through these questions.

1. Who comes to mind immediately when you think about forgiveness? Why do you think that is?

2. What feels hardest about forgiving this person, the pain, the injustice, or the lack of apology?

3. Have you been waiting for your feelings to change before choosing to forgive? What has that cost you?

4. How has holding onto unforgiveness affected your peace, your joy, or your relationship with God?

5. What would it look like to choose forgiveness today, even if your emotions don't fully align yet?

Chapter 20

Forgiveness For Freedom

Matthew 6:14-15

Forgiveness brings you freedom. Matthew 6:14-15 says it this way, "If you forgive those who sin against you, your heavenly Father will forgive you. But if you refuse to forgive others, your Father will not forgive your sins."

Ouch. This is one of those verses that doesn't leave any room for man's interpretation. It is what it is. Jesus is crystal clear: our willingness to forgive is directly tied to our relationship with God. That doesn't mean you earn God's forgiveness by forgiving others; it means that an unforgiving heart is out of step with the God who forgave you first.

Forgiveness is less about the other person and more about your own spiritual health.

When you hold onto bitterness, it's like putting up a wall between you and God. You're not hurting your ex as much as you're hurting yourself.

Here's the freeing part: forgiveness doesn't require you to have warm, fuzzy feelings toward the person. You can forgive and still have boundaries. You can forgive and never see them again. The point is to take your hands off their throat and put them into God's hands instead.

Let's Pray Together

Father,

This is hard. You're asking me to release something that feels justified to hold onto. But I don't want anything to stand between me and You. I don't want bitterness to take root in my heart or block what You're doing in my life. So today, I choose to forgive. Not because it's easy, but because I want to walk in alignment with You. Help me let go of what I've been gripping tightly. And when I feel tempted to pick it back up, remind me that I've already placed it in Your hands. Give me the strength to keep choosing freedom.

In Jesus' name,

Amen.

Sit With These Scriptures

"If you forgive those who sin against you, your heavenly Father will forgive you..." Matthew 6:14–15

"Let all bitterness and wrath and anger... be put away from you... forgiving one another, as God in Christ forgave you." Ephesians 4:31–32

SIT IN THAT TRUTH
FORGIVENESS FOR FREEDOM

Take a few moments to ask God to remove any distractions and to silence your own voice and the enemy's voice, so that you can hear God clearly and focus on Him. Invite the Holy Spirit to help you as you work through these questions.

1. When you read Matthew 6:14–15, what is your honest reaction—resistance, conviction, frustration, surrender?

2. Is there someone you know you've been unwilling (or not ready) to forgive? What's been holding you back?

3. How might unforgiveness be affecting your relationship with God right now?

4. Do you believe forgiveness means reconciliation or removing boundaries? Why or why not?

5. What would it look like today to take your hands off the situation and place it fully into God's hands

Chapter 21

Boundaries Are Biblical

Proverbs 22:3

The wise see danger and take refuge; that is a healthy boundary. Proverbs 22:3 says, "The prudent see danger and take refuge, but the simple keep going and pay the penalty."

Let's get something straight: God is not glorified by you staying in a relationship that's toxic, abusive, or chronically unsafe. Sometimes the most obedient thing you can do is leave. And yes, that can happen even in a marriage.

This isn't about quitting when it gets hard; marriage is full of seasons that require grit and commitment. But there's a difference between working through struggles and staying in harm's way. God gives us wisdom and discernment for a reason. He warns us when danger is ahead, and sometimes He opens the door for us to walk out.

If God has led you out, that doesn't mean you failed. It might mean you finally listened. And if you've ever wrestled with the guilt of "But God hates divorce," remember this: He hates what destroys His children even more. His heart for you is life, not constant survival mode.

Let's Pray Together

Father,

Thank You for being a God of wisdom, not confusion. Thank You that

You care about my safety, my healing, and my wholeness. Help me to recognize where You are leading me. Give me clarity to see what is healthy and what is not. Where I've ignored warning signs or stayed longer than I should have, bring understanding and grace. And where You are calling me to step away or set boundaries, give me the courage to follow You. Remind me that obedience sometimes looks like walking away. And that choosing safety and healing is not failure, but faith.

In Jesus' name,

Amen.

Sit With These Scriptures

"The prudent see danger and take refuge, but the simple keep going and pay the penalty." Proverbs 22:3

"For God is not a God of confusion but of peace." 1 Corinthians 14:33

SIT IN THAT TRUTH
BOUNDARIES ARE BIBLICAL

Take a few moments to ask God to remove any distractions and to silence your own voice and the enemy's voice, so that you can hear God clearly and focus on Him. Invite the Holy Spirit to help you as you work through these questions.

1. Have you ever confused forgiveness with staying in a harmful or unhealthy situation? What did that look like?

2. Are there areas in your life where you sense God prompting you toward safety, distance, or stronger boundaries?

3. What fears or beliefs make it hard for you to step away from what you know isn't healthy?

4. Do you tend to ignore red flags or warning signs? What have you learned from past experiences?

5. What would it look like to trust God's wisdom and follow His leading, even when it's difficult or misunderstood by others?

HARD TRUTH #8
YOUR CALLING IS NOT CANCELED BY DIVORCE

Here's something the enemy would love for you to believe: divorce means you're done. That somehow your "real" purpose expired with your marriage certificate. And, that your mistakes, your pain, and your current status have somehow bumped you down from God's "called" list down to the "maybe someday" list.

But here's the truth: your calling didn't start with your spouse, and it doesn't end with your divorce. God didn't design your purpose around someone else's faithfulness, maturity, or willingness to honor the covenant. He wrote your calling before you were even born (Jeremiah 1:5), and He doesn't go back and erase it because your story didn't unfold the way you thought it would.

Yes, divorce changes things: your rhythm, your finances, your home, and sometimes your friend group. But it doesn't change who God says you are or what He has for you to do. The Bible is full of people whose callings were activated in the middle of what looked like the messiest seasons of their lives. Joseph stepped into his destiny after betrayal and prison. Ruth's story unfolded after widowhood. Paul's ministry began after years of persecuting the very church he would lead.

Your divorce may have taken you on an unexpected detour, but it's not a dead end. God can (and will) weave even this section into your Kingdom assignment. In this section, you will learn that the very thing you thought disqualified you may become the very testimony that equips you to lead others to freedom.

Chapter 22

God's Plans Remain

Jeremiah 29:11

God's plans are good and He declares, "For I know the plans I have for you," says the Lord. "They are plans for good and not for disaster, to give you a future and a hope." (Jeremiah 29:11 NLT)

We tend to quote this verse like it's a motivational Instagram caption, but the context is much deeper. God spoke these words to His people while they were living in exile, far from home, far from comfort, and far from the life they thought they'd have. In other words, they were in a place they never planned to be. Sound familiar?

Divorce can feel like exile, like you've been pushed into a new life you didn't choose, surrounded by unknowns you don't know how to navigate. And yet, God's message to you is the same as it was to His people then: My plans for you haven't changed.

This doesn't mean every detail of your life will go back to the way you imagined. It means His purpose for you isn't contingent on you staying in the same relationship, the same house, or the same season forever. He knows where you are, He knows what's next, and He knows how to get you there, even if you can't see more than one step ahead right now.

Let's Pray Together

Father,

Thank You that Your plans for me have not changed. Even when my life looks different than I expected, You are still good, and You are still leading me. Help me to trust You in the unknown. When I feel uncertain about the future, remind me that You already see it clearly. Where I've believed lies that I've missed my chance or disqualified myself, replace those thoughts with Your truth. Give me faith to believe that You are still working, still guiding, and still preparing something good ahead of me. Teach me to walk forward one step at a time, trusting that You are establishing my path.

In Jesus' name,

Amen.

Sit With These Scriptures

"For I know the plans I have for you... plans for good and not for disaster, to give you a future and a hope." Jeremiah 29:11

"The heart of man plans his way, but the Lord establishes his steps." Proverbs 16:9

SIT IN THAT TRUTH
GOD'S PLANS REMAIN

Take a few moments to ask God to remove any distractions and to silence your own voice and the enemy's voice, so that you can hear God clearly and focus on Him. Invite the Holy Spirit to help you as you work through these questions.

1. Where in your life does it feel like things didn't go according to plan?

2. Have you believed, even subtly, that your current situation has disqualified you from God's best?

3. What fears come up when you think about your future after divorce?

4. Do you trust that God's plans are still good, even if they look different than you expected? Why or why not?

5. What would it look like to take one step forward in faith, even if you can't see the full picture yet?

Chapter 23

Purpose In Every Season

Ecclesiastes 3:1

There is a purpose and a time for everything under the sun. Ecclesiastes 3:1 says it this way, "For everything there is a season, a time for every activity under heaven."

When life changes suddenly, it's tempting to label entire seasons as "wasted." You might look back on your marriage and think, All that time, for what? Or you might see this current stage of healing as a holding pattern, like you're just waiting until you feel whole again before you can really "get back to life."

But the Kingdom doesn't work that way. God isn't limited to your "good" seasons. He's just as active in the quiet, tear-streaked, uncertain ones. In fact, those might be the very seasons where He does His deepest work.

The wilderness may feel like punishment, but biblically, it's often the place where God reveals Himself most clearly. The Israelites saw His provision in the desert. Jesus overcame temptation there. And you? You might just find that the season you wanted to rush through is the season that prepared you for your next assignment.

So instead of asking, "When will this be over?" start asking, "God, what do You want to show me here?" You may find that purpose has been woven into the waiting all along.

Let's Pray Together

Father,

Thank You that no season of my life is wasted in Your hands. Even the ones I don't understand, the ones that feel slow or painful, You are still at work. Help me to see this season through Your eyes. Not as something to rush through, but as something You are using to shape me. Open my eyes to the growth, lessons, and opportunities right in front of me. And give me the patience to trust that You are preparing me for what's ahead. Teach me to be present with You here, knowing that You are just as active in this season as in any other.

In Jesus' name,

Amen.

Sit With These Scriptures

"For everything there is a season, a time for every activity under heaven." Ecclesiastes 3:1

"And we know that for those who love God all things work together for good..." Romans 8:28

SIT IN THAT TRUTH
PURPOSE IN EVERY SEASON

Take a few moments to ask God to remove any distractions and to silence your own voice and the enemy's voice, so that you can hear God clearly and focus on Him. Invite the Holy Spirit to help you as you work through these questions.

1. What season of life do you find yourself in right now, and how have you been viewing it?

2. Have you labeled any part of your story as "wasted"? What makes you feel that way?

3. Are you waiting to feel fully healed before stepping back into purpose or calling? Why?

4. Where might God be working in your life right now that you've been overlooking?

5. What would it look like to embrace this season instead of rushing through it?

Chapter 24

God's Glory Through Your Story

Romans 8:28

Your life can still bear fruit. Let's revisit Romans chapter 8, but this time in the context of God working through your story.

"And we know that God causes everything to work together for the good of those who love God and are called according to His purpose." (Romans 8:28 NLT)

Let's clear this up: this verse does not mean everything that happens to you is good. It means God can take anything, even the painful, unjust, or downright unfair, and work it for good. Divorce is not good. Betrayal is not good. The nights you cried until your chest hurt are not good. But the God who parted seas, fed thousands with scraps, and turned death into resurrection? He's more than capable of bringing good out of your worst moments.

Here's the kicker: that "good" isn't always about making you comfortable again. It's about making you more like Christ, deepening your faith, and giving your story power to help others. Your scars may become the evidence someone else needs to believe God can heal them, too.

When you hand your story over to Him, the whole thing, even the parts you wish you could erase, you give Him permission to turn it into a weapon against the enemy. And when the enemy tries to use your divorce to shame you, God can flip it and use it to set someone else free. That's redemption!

Let's Pray Together

Father,

Thank You that nothing in my story is wasted. Even the parts that were painful, confusing, or unfair, You are able to redeem. Help me to trust You with the whole story. Not just the polished parts, but the broken ones too. Give me the courage to see my story the way You see it, not as something to hide, but as something You can use. And when the time is right, give me boldness to share it in a way that points others back to You. Use my life for Your glory. Take what was meant for harm and turn it into something that brings healing, hope, and freedom to others.

In Jesus' name,

Amen.

Sit With These Scriptures

"And we know that God causes everything to work together for the good of those who love God..." Romans 8:28

"They triumphed over him by the blood of the Lamb and by the word of their testimony..." Revelation 12:11

SIT IN THAT TRUTH
GOD'S GLORY THROUGH YOUR STORY

Take a few moments to ask God to remove any distractions and to silence your own voice and the enemy's voice, so that you can hear God clearly and focus on Him. Invite the Holy Spirit to help you as you work through these questions.

1. What part of your story have you felt tempted to hide or minimize? Why?

2. Do you believe God can truly use your pain to help someone else, or does that feel hard to accept?

3. How has your perspective on Romans 8:28 changed as you've walked through your own story?

4. In what ways has God already brought growth, strength, or deeper faith through your hardest moments?

5. What would it look like to offer your story to God as something He can use for His glory?

HOPE TRUTH #1
THE RESTORATION BEGINS

WHEW. We made it. We've walked through the hard truths, the messy emotions, the deep heart work, and maybe a few moments where you wanted to slam this book shut because I said something you didn't want to hear (it's okay, I still love you). But here you are, still reading, still standing, still showing up. That, my friend, is victory.

This is the part where we shift gears. We're moving from just surviving to living again. From staring at the rubble to seeing the rebuild. From pain that once felt like it would never end to hope that stirs your heart once more. So, take a deep breath, unclench your jaw, and open your heart. In this section, we will see the beauty of grace, joy, peace, strength, and unshakable hope that He's been working on behind the scenes all along.

Chapter 25

God Restores Years Lost

Joel 2:25

God is into restoring what was lost and stolen. Joel 2:25 says, "I will give you back what you lost to the swarming locusts." (Joel 2:25 NLT)

If there's one thing divorce can make you feel, it's robbed. Robbed of years. Robbed of joy. Robbed of the life you pictured when you said, "I do." The enemy loves this because, if he can get you to believe that those years were wasted, he can keep you from believing God can redeem them. But Joel 2:25 tells a different story. God looks at His people after devastation and says, "I will give you back what you lost." Not "I'll help you forget about it," not "I'll make you numb so you won't care." He says, restore.

Now, let's be real: restoration in God's economy doesn't always mean you get back exactly what you had. This isn't about Him rewinding the tape of your life so you can replay it the "right" way. This is about Him taking the years that feel empty and filling them with something so full you'll shake your head, wondering how you ever lived without it. It might not look like your old dream; in fact, it probably won't, but it will carry His fingerprints, and it will be better than what you could have pieced together on your own. Think about Ruth. She lost her husband, her home, and her future plans. But she stayed faithful to the God she had come to know, and He wove her into the lineage of Jesus. Did she get her old life back? No. Did she get something better? Absolutely. That's the way God works: He trades ashes for beauty, despair for joy, broken pieces for Kingdom purpose.

And here's where the sass meets the sanctification: you can't keep staring at the loss and expect to see the restoration. God is asking you to trust Him enough to let go of all the "should have beens" and open your hands for the "better than I imagined." That's not easy, I know, but you cannot walk into the restored future He's offering while you're still clinging to the ruins of the past.

Let's Pray Together

Father,

Thank You that You are a God who restores. Nothing in my life is beyond Your reach, not the years I feel were lost, not the pain I still carry. Help me release what I thought my life would look like. Give me the courage to let go of the "should have been" and trust You with what is. Teach me to believe that You are still working, still restoring, still writing something good. Even when I don't see it yet. Open my hands to receive what You have for me now. And remind me that Your version of restoration is always better than anything I could have held onto.

In Jesus' name,

Amen.

Sit With These Scriptures

"To give them beauty for ashes, the oil of joy for mourning..." Isaiah 61:3

"And we know that for those who love God all things work together for good..." Romans 8:28

SIT IN THAT TRUTH
GOD RESTORES YEARS LOST

Take a few moments to ask God to remove any distractions and to silence your own voice and the enemy's voice, so that you can hear God clearly and focus on Him. Invite the Holy Spirit to help you as you work through these questions.

1. What "loss" have you been replaying in your mind that has kept you stuck looking backward instead of trusting God for what's ahead?

2. Where have you believed the lie that those years were wasted instead of surrendered to God for redemption?

3. What would it look like for you to release the "should have been" version of your life and open your hands to what God is doing now?

4. How has God already begun restoring something in you, even if it doesn't look like what you expected?

5. Do you trust that God's version of restoration is better than your version of what was lost? Why or why not?

Chapter 26

Joy Will Return

Psalm 126:5

There may be tears now, but one day there will be joy. "Those who plant in tears will harvest with shouts of joy." (Psalm 126:5 NLT)

Let's just go ahead and say it, sometimes joy feels like the furthest thing from possible after divorce. You're standing in the middle of what feels like emotional rubble, and someone dares to tell you, "joy is coming." Really? When? How? What's left to even feel joyful about?

But Psalm 126:5 reminds us that tears are not wasted. They're seeds. That means every sleepless night, every moment your chest ached from crying, every silent drive where you replayed conversations in your head, God can take even that and turn it into a harvest of joy. And here's the kicker: joy in God's economy isn't a fake smile or a "positive vibes only" mindset. It's deep, rooted, unshakable confidence that God is still good, still sovereign, still writing the story, even when the plot twist broke your heart.

Think about it: seeds must be buried before they can grow. That means part of the reason you can't see the joy yet is that it's still underground, still germinating in the dark, and breaking open where nobody can see it. That doesn't mean it's not working. It means it's not ready to sprout, yet. But when it does, that joy will be richer because of the pain that planted it.

So yes, friend, you will laugh again without feeling guilty. You will find moments of delight that don't feel forced. You'll stand in the sunlight of God's goodness and realize the heaviness has lifted, and it will make sense why Scripture says your mourning will turn into dancing.

Let's Pray Together

Father,

Thank You that my tears are not wasted. You see every single one, and You are doing something with them. When joy feels far away, remind me that You are still near. That even in this season, You are working beneath the surface in ways I can't yet see. Help me trust that joy will return. Not forced or fake, but real, deep, and rooted in You. Give me the ability to notice the small moments of light. The reminders that You are still good, still present, still faithful. And when joy begins to rise again, help me receive it without guilt, knowing it's a gift from you.

In Jesus' name,

Amen.

Sit With These Scriptures

"Weeping may endure for a night, but joy comes in the morning." Psalm 30:5

"You will grieve, but your grief will turn to joy." John 16:20

SIT IN THAT TRUTH
JOY WILL RETURN

Take a few moments to ask God to remove any distractions and to silence your own voice and the enemy's voice, so that you can hear God clearly and focus on Him. Invite the Holy Spirit to help you as you work through these questions.

1. Where have you convinced yourself that joy is no longer possible for you?

2. What tears have you cried that you've labeled as pointless instead of planted?

3. How might God be using this season, even now, to grow something you can't yet see?

4. What would it look like to give yourself permission to experience joy again without guilt?

5. Can you trust that God is working beneath the surface, even when you don't feel it yet? Why or why not?

Chapter 27

Peace That Surpasses Understanding

Philippians 4:6-7

God can guard your heart and mind when you surrender to Him. The Bible says, "Do not be anxious about anything, but in every situation, by prayer and petition, with thanksgiving, present your requests to God. And the peace of God, which transcends all understanding, will guard your hearts and your minds in Christ Jesus. (Philippians 4:6-7 NLT)

There's peace you can explain, like when the bills are paid, the kids are doing well, and life feels stable. And then there's the kind Paul is talking about here: peace that makes no earthly sense. The kind that lets you breathe when circumstances scream panic. The kind that whispers, "You're okay. Gods got this," even when the situation hasn't changed.

Here's the beautiful part: this peace doesn't come from figuring everything out; it comes from surrender. The moment you stop white-knuckling your way through life and slide your worries across the table to God, His peace starts standing guard. And yes, guard, like a soldier at the gate of your heart and mind, saying, "Fear, anxiety, lies, you aren't allowed in here."

I won't sugarcoat it: you may have to hand the same worry back to Him 20 times in one day. But every time you do, you're building a habit of choosing peace over panic. And one day, you'll look back and realize what used to unravel you now barely rattles you. That's what His peace does, it transforms you from the inside out.

Let's Pray Together

Father,

Thank You that Your peace is not dependent on my circumstances. That even when things feel uncertain, You are steady. You see the thoughts that keep circling, the worries I keep picking back up. Help me to release them to You repeatedly if necessary. Teach me to trust You more than I trust my fears. To fix my mind on You instead of everything that feels out of control. Guard my heart and my mind with Your peace. The kind that doesn't always make sense, but holds me steady anyway. Remind me that I don't have to carry this. You've already made a way for me to walk in peace.

In Jesus' name,

Amen.

Sit With These Scriptures

"You keep him in perfect peace whose mind is stayed on you, because he trusts in you." Isaiah 26:3

"Peace I leave with you; My peace I give to you... Let not your hearts be troubled, neither let them be afraid." John 14:27

SIT IN THAT TRUTH
PEACE THAT SURPASSES UNDERSTANDING

Take a few moments to ask God to remove any distractions and to silence your own voice and the enemy's voice, so that you can hear God clearly and focus on Him. Invite the Holy Spirit to help you as you work through these questions.

1. What worries have been sitting heavy on your mind that you've been trying to carry on your own?

2. Where have you been trying to figure everything out instead of surrendering it to God?

3. What would it look like for you to truly hand those things over to Him, not just once, but continually?

4. How has anxiety or fear been affecting your ability to trust God in this season?

5. Do you believe God's peace is available to you right now, even if your circumstances haven't changed? Why or why not?

HOPE TRUTH # 2
THE STRENGTH TO RISE

I have one more truth for you...healing isn't the finish line, it's the foundation.

You've done the hard work. You've faced what hurt, released what needed to go, and allowed God to begin restoring what was broken. But now? Now comes the part where you live from it. Where what God has done in you starts showing up through you.

Because at some point, you must get back up. Not in your own strength, not in a rushed or forced way, but in the steady, Spirit-filled strength that only God provides. The kind that meets you on the days you feel strong and the days you don't. The kind that doesn't just help you survive but equips you to move forward.

In this section, we're stepping into that strength. The kind that renews when you're tired, anchors you when life feels uncertain, and gives you the courage to turn the page and walk into what God is making new. This isn't about pretending everything is okay. It's about knowing that even when everything isn't, He still is.

So, if you've been waiting for a sign that you're ready to move forward, this is it. Not because everything is perfect, but because God is faithful.

Take a breath. Lift your head.

It's time to rise.

Chapter 28

Strength To Keep Going

Isaiah 40:31

Renewed strength for the journey is yours as you trust in Him. "Those who trust in the Lord will find new strength. They will soar high on wings like eagles..." (Isaiah 40:31 NLT)

Some days you feel unstoppable. Other days, you're fortunate if you get out of bed and remember to eat. Both are valid. God's promise in Isaiah isn't that you'll always feel strong; it's that when you trust Him, He will renew your strength. That means you can run out and still get refilled.

Eagle imagery is no accident here. Eagles don't constantly flap their wings to stay in the air; they soar by catching the right wind currents. It's less about frantic movement and more about positioning themselves in what's carrying them. That's your job, to position yourself in God's presence so His Spirit does the heavy lifting.

And here's some tough love: renewing strength often means slowing down enough for God to pour it in. If you're always running at burnout speed trying to "handle it," you'll miss the refill. Let Him be your source instead of your backup plan.

Let's Pray Together

Father,

Thank You that I don't have to rely on my own strength. When I feel tired, overwhelmed, or worn down, You are still my source. You see the places where I've been pushing, striving, and trying to hold it all together. Help me to slow down and come back to You. Teach me to trust that You will give me exactly what I need for today. Not all at once, not for every future moment, but for right now. Fill me with Your strength where I feel weak. Remind me that I don't have to carry this on my own. Help me to rest in You, to depend on You, and to move forward in the strength that only You provide. For when I am weak, Lord, You are strong.

In Jesus' name,

Amen.

Sit With These Scriptures

"My grace is sufficient for you, for my power is made perfect in weakness." 2 Corinthians 12:9

"God is our refuge and strength, a very present help in trouble." Psalm 46:1

SIT IN THAT TRUTH
STRENGTH TO KEEP GOING

Take a few moments to ask God to remove any distractions and to silence your own voice and the enemy's voice, so that you can hear God clearly and focus on Him. Invite the Holy Spirit to help you as you work through these questions.

1. Where are you feeling the most tired right now, physically, emotionally, or spiritually?

2. In what areas have you been trying to push through in your own strength instead of depending on God?

3. What would it look like for you to slow down and position yourself in God's presence today?

4. Where might God be inviting you to trust Him instead of trying to "handle it" on your own?

5. Do you believe God will give you the strength you need for each day? Why or why?

Chapter 29

Unshakeable Hope

Hebrews 10:23

Hold on without wavering because God can be trusted. His Word says, "Let us hold tightly without wavering to the hope we affirm, for God can be trusted to keep His promise." (Hebrews 10:23 NLT)

Hope is not wishful thinking. It's not crossing your fingers and hoping life doesn't fall apart again. Hope is a fierce, steady grip on the truth that God's promises are more certain than your circumstances.

Let's be honest, hope can feel risky when you've been let down. But here's the difference: when your hope is anchored in people or situations, it will always be shaky. When it's anchored in God's unchanging character, it's unshakeable. The winds can howl, the waves can crash, but the anchor holds.

This verse isn't telling you to "cheer up." It's telling you to hold on tight to what you know is true: God keeps His word. Every time. So even if you don't see the outcome yet, you can live today like it's already settled because in Heaven's eyes, it is.

Let's Pray Together

Father,

Thank You that my hope is not in people or circumstances, but in You. You are steady, unchanging, and always faithful. You see the places where I've been hesitant to hope again. The places where disappointment has made me hold back. Help me to trust You again. To anchor my hope in who You are, not in what I see. Remind me that Your promises are still true. That which You have spoken, You will fulfill. When doubt tries to creep in, help me hold tightly to the truth. To stand firm, even when I don't yet see the outcome. Fill me with a hope that is steady, confident, and rooted in You.

In Jesus' name,

Amen.

Sit With These Scriptures

"The steadfast love of the Lord never ceases; his mercies never come to an end; they are new every morning..." Lamentations 3:22–23

"May the God of hope fill you with all joy and peace in believing..." Romans 15:13

SIT IN THAT TRUTH
UNSHAKEABLE HOPE

Take a few moments to ask God to remove any distractions and to silence your own voice and the enemy's voice, so that you can hear God clearly and focus on Him. Invite the Holy Spirit to help you as you work through these questions.

1. Where have you felt hesitant to hope again because of past disappointment?

2. What have you been anchoring your hope in that keeps shifting or failing you?

3. What does it look like for you to hold tightly to God's promises, even when you don't see the outcome yet?

4. Where is doubt trying to creep in and challenge what you know to be true about God?

5. Do you truly believe God can be trusted to keep His promises in your life? Why or why not?

Chapter 30

A New Chapter Begins

Revelation 21:5

God makes all things brand new, and a new beginning is yours. His Word says, "Look, I am making everything new!" (Revelation 21:5 NLT) This is your moment to exhale.

The old chapter, with all its pain, loss, and confusion, is not the whole story. God Himself says He is making everything new. He doesn't erase the past; He redeems it and uses it to build what's next.

Here's the thing about new chapters: they require you to turn the page. You can't keep rereading the old one and expect to move forward. God is inviting you to step into what He's writing now, and spoiler alert: it's good.

So yes, you've been through a lot. Yes, you're still healing. But this is the point in the story where your scars become testimonies, your setbacks become setups, and your survival becomes a platform for His glory. This is not just about a fresh start, it's about walking into a future designed by the Author who already knows the ending, and spoiler alert: it's beautiful.

Let's Pray Together

Father,

Thank You for making all things new. Not just around me, but within me. Thank You that my story is not over. That which is ahead is still being written by Your hands. Help me release the past fully into Your care. Not ignoring it but trusting You with it. Give me the courage to step forward with hope. To believe that what You have for me is good. Open my eyes to what You are doing right now. And lead me into this next chapter with confidence, peace, and trust in You.

In Jesus' name,

Amen.

Sit With These Scriptures

"See, I am doing a new thing! Now it springs up; do you not perceive it?" Isaiah 43:19

"Therefore, if anyone is in Christ, he is a new creation..." 2 Corinthians 5:17

SIT IN THAT TRUTH
A NEW CHAPTER BEGINS

Take a few moments to ask God to remove any distractions and to silence your own voice and the enemy's voice, so that you can hear God clearly and focus on Him. Invite the Holy Spirit to help you as you work through these questions.

1. What is one thing you're genuinely excited about as you step into this next chapter?

2. What would it look like to believe that something good is ahead of you?

3. What is one small step you can take today that reflects the new life God is building?

4. How has God already begun making something new in you?

5. If you fully trusted God with your future, how would you walk differently starting today?

Chapter 31

The Rise After The Rubble

Philippians 4:13

Look at you. You made it. " You can do all things through Christ who gives you strength." Philippians 4:13

At the beginning of this journey, you may have opened these pages with your heart in pieces, your hope barely breathing, and your mind wondering if you would ever really feel whole again. And yet, here you are. Wiser. Stronger. Softer in the right places. More anchored in truth than when you began.

You did the hard work. You faced truths you might have wanted to avoid. You allowed God to search your heart, challenge old patterns, and begin rebuilding what was broken. And even if some places are still tender, you can sense it now. New life is forming where there was once only loss.

That, my friend, is victory. This is not the end. It is a turning point.

You've seen what God can restore.

You've felt the strength He provides.

And now, you're stepping into a life no longer defined by what fell apart, but by what He is building.

Your story does not stop at survival. It moves forward into wholeness. Into wisdom. Into a life marked by purpose and anchored in truth. Divorce may be part of your story, but it is no longer the headline. Redemption is.

There will be more growth ahead, more healing, and more refining. But there will also be more peace, clarity, and purpose than before. God wastes nothing, not the pain, not the waiting, not even the mistakes. He is faithful to complete the work He began in you.

So, take this moment and breathe. The divorce did not defeat you. It did not disqualify you. It did not cancel your calling. It refined you, revealed you, and positioned you to rise. Your next chapter isn't something you have to strive to create. It's something you get to walk into with God. The truth you carry with you now, the truth that you are now grounded in, and that is, you may be divorced, but you are not defeated!

Keep walking. Keep trusting. Keep rising.

With love,

Ruby

About The *Author*

Ruby Crotty is a Christian leader, mentor, speaker, and founder of The Waves Collective, a ministry focused on identity, healing, and purpose after divorce. After 18 years in the corporate world, she stepped into a new calling in ministry and leadership, helping others rebuild their lives through biblical truth and discipleship. She is known for her bold truth, deep faith, and unwavering belief that God still restores what was once broken.

Ruby lives in Florida with her two amazing children. When she's not mentoring or writing, she enjoys exploring local coffee shops with friends, spending time poolside with a book in hand, paddleboarding the waterways of Northeast Florida, and serving at her church home, where her faith continues to deepen in community.

"'Little girl, I say to you, arise.'"
Mark 5:41 (ESV)

Your story doesn't end *here*

ESTD 2026

WAVES
COLLECTIVE

The Waves Collective is a faith-based community helping people rebuild after divorce through biblical truth, healing, discipleship, and authentic community.

Join the Community

Stay Connected. Find Resources

www.thewavescollective.org

@the_waves_co

hello@thewavescollective.org

Connect with *Ruby*

@rubycrotty

"Mightier than the thunders of many waters,
mightier than the waves of the sea,
the Lord on high is mighty!"
Psalm 93:4 (ESV)

Made in the USA
Coppell, TX
10 June 2026

80131683R00089